EAST ANGLIAN BUSES
1970 TO 1995

ROBERT APPLETON

AMBERLEY

Front cover: Delivered in 1969, 3000 (CPU 979G) was numerically Eastern National's first Bristol VRT/SL6G with an Eastern Coach Works seventy-seat body. On 17 April 1982, 3000 was allocated to Harwich, and had just arrived at Harwich bus station on service 122 from Ramsey. In the background is the High Lighthouse, built in 1818 – a prominent feature of maritime Harwich.

Rear cover: Eastern Counties service revisions from 30 April 1972 included service 209, Ipswich–East Bergholt, which was rerouted in East Bergholt and extended to Manningtree and Mistley. The first service 209 to reach Mistley on this date was worked by RLE869 (WPW 869H), a Bristol RELL6G that was new in 1970 with fifty semi-coach seats in her Eastern Coach Works body. There are images in this book of RLE869 in her original coach livery, and later in National Bus Company livery.

First published 2018

Amberley Publishing
The Hill, Stroud
Gloucestershire, GL5 4EP

www.amberley-books.com

Copyright © Robert Appleton, 2018

The right of Robert Appleton to be identified as the Author of this work has been asserted in accordance with the Copyrights, Designs and Patents Act 1988.

ISBN 978 1 4456 7386 8 (print)
ISBN 978 1 4456 7387 5 (ebook)

British Library Cataloguing in Publication Data.
A catalogue record for this book is available from the British Library.

Typesetting by Amberley Publishing.
Printed in the UK.

Introduction

My father was a keen amateur photographer. In 1969 he obtained a second-hand Exacta 35 mm camera for me. The results with this camera were a great improvement on anything I had achieved before, so from 1970 onwards I was able to combine my enthusiasm for buses with photography.

There are various definitions of East Anglia, but for the purpose of this book I have used north-east Essex, Suffolk, Norfolk, and Cambridgeshire, including Peterborough.

Traveling to school in Colchester from Mistley meant using the buses of the Eastern Counties Omnibus Co. Ltd, operating from East Bergholt outstation. Visits to Ipswich by bus on Saturdays or during school holidays revealed a network of services connecting the smaller towns and villages of east Suffolk to Ipswich. As well as the main Ipswich depot, there were smaller depots at Felixstowe and Saxmundham, plus a number of outstations where anything from one to six buses were garaged overnight.

The outstation system worked very well, reducing dead mileage and giving employment to local people. Normally, the first bus in the morning from a village in to Ipswich, and the last bus from Ipswich at the end of the day, would be an outstation bus. Duties were arranged so that the outstation buses were refuelled and cleaned during the day at the Foundation Street depot in Ipswich.

In 1970 Eastern Counties was part of the National Bus Company, but the buses were still in Tilling livery. The National Bus Company corporate livery did not start to appear until the end of 1972.

As the 1970s progressed, one-man operation spread and crew operation declined, so trips were made to Cambridge, Peterborough, and Norwich to see Bristol/Eastern Coach Works Lodekkas working city services before crew operation finished completely in the early 1980s. The spread of one-man operation was helped by downgrading Bristol LS5G and MW5G coaches to stage carriage operation.

Innovations in the 1980s included the network of Eastline limited-stop services and joint limited-stop services with London Country, connecting Cambridge with London.

Eastern Counties was split up in September 1984, leaving the company with bus operations in Norfolk and Suffolk. After bus deregulation in October 1986, and privatisation in February 1987, a new Post Office red livery gradually replaced the National Bus Company poppy red.

Eastern Counties became part of Grampian Regional Transport Holdings in July 1994, which brought about a cream-based livery. Then, almost a year later, the merger with Badgerline took place in June 1995 to form the FirstBus Group.

Mistley was also served by the Eastern National Omnibus Company Ltd, another Tilling company that became part of the National Bus Company in 1969. Eastern National had less need of outstations than Eastern Counties, but Eastern National had a small depot at Harwich. While Harwich had its own allocation, buses were often interchanged with the larger depot at Clacton, so Harwich was always worth a visit.

If I wanted to see more Eastern National buses, then Colchester was easily reached by bus from Mistley.

An innovation in the early 1980s was the network of Highwayman limited-stop services that connected Essex with towns and cities in neighbouring counties.

The Eastern National livery changed from Tilling green to National Bus Company leaf green, and in preparation for deregulation and privatisation, a new dark green and yellow livery was introduced. After Eastern National became part of the Badgerline Group in April 1990 a brighter green and yellow livery was introduced, complete with a smiling badger on each side of the bus. In June 1995 Badgerline merged with GRT Holdings to create FirstBus Group, bringing Eastern National and Eastern Counties back in to common ownership.

Also to be seen in East Anglia were the buses of two other former Tilling companies that were part of the National Bus Company: Lincolnshire Road Car Company buses reached Kings Lynn and Peterborough, while United Counties Omnibus Company buses reached Cambridge and Peterborough.

I regret that I did not go to Lowestoft in time to see the Waveney municipal buses before closure in 1977, but I did photograph the municipal buses of Great Yarmouth, Colchester and Ipswich.

I also followed some of the independent operators in East Anglia. This included the immaculate buses of Delaine, who operated in to Peterborough from Bourne in Lincolnshire, and still do so today. In Suffolk there was Bickers of Coddenham, who made a success of operating rural bus services into Ipswich that had been given up by Eastern Counties. Then there were independents that operated on both sides of the Essex/Suffolk border: Norfolk's of Nayland, Chambers of Bures, Hedingham & District and Carters Coach Services.

Reverting to September 1984, Ambassador Travel took over the coach operations of Eastern Counties, and Cambus took over the bus services in the western (mainly Cambridgeshire) area of Eastern Counties. In September 1989 the Peterborough area of Cambus became the Viscount Bus & Coach Company, introducing another new livery. In December 1995 Cambus and Viscount became part of Stagecoach Group. The advent of the large bus groups of First Bus and Stagecoach would have a profound effect on bus services in East Anglia. As a result, this book concludes in 1995.

In the period before the deregulation of bus services in 1986, minibus networks were introduced in urban areas. I am afraid this development passed me by, as I was more interested in full-sized buses. For example, Eastern Counties, Eastern National, Cambus and Viscount all purchased second-hand Bristol VRTs with Eastern Coach Works bodies.

I hope that the images in this book have captured the essential character of bus operations in East Anglia, especially the rural services connecting the villages and small towns with the larger towns and cities.

Special thanks are due to my wife, Rosemary, for her support during the preparation of this book.

Eastern Counties LKD178 (UNG 178) at Ipswich Old Cattle Market bus station in August 1971. New in 1956, LKD178 was a Bristol LD5G with an Eastern Coach Works sixty-seat body. In 1971 she was one of the few buses allocated to Ipswich with intermediate points on the destination blind.

Bristol LD5G LKD202 (VVF 202) was new to Eastern Counties in 1958. In October 1971 she was working from East Bergholt outstation on the 14.00 Colchester–Ipswich 221 service, in Harwich Road, Mistley.

Eastern Counties LFS31 (2931 PW), a Bristol FS5G, was new in 1962, and like all members of the LFS class, the Eastern Coach Works body had sixty seats. In May 1970 LFS31 was working the 10.10 Ipswich–Clacton 123 service, in Harwich Road, Mistley, taking a happy load of passengers heading for the Essex coast at Clacton. Service 123 was jointly operated with Eastern National.

LFS76 (AAH 614B), a Bristol FS5G that was new in 1964, is seen on a layover at Ipswich Old Cattle Market bus station in August 1971 while working from Stradbroke outstation. LFS76 was one of the first buses at Ipswich depot to have its destination blind masked, in order to take a new blind with all destinations listed in alphabetical order.

Eastern Counties LM933 (WPW 633), a Bristol LS5G with an Eastern Coach Works forty-five-seat body new in 1957, is seen at East Bergholt outstation in August 1970. The left-hand side of the outstation building could accommodate low-height double-deckers, while the right-hand side was restricted to single-deckers.

Eastern Counties LC559 (6559 AH), a Bristol SC4LK with an Eastern Coach Works thirty-five seat body, was new in 1959. In May 1970, LC559 was working from East Bergholt outstation on a Sunday duty – the 16.50 East Bergholt–Colchester 221 service – in Harwich Road, Mistley.

Timetable and duty changes from 17 May 1970 brought a seventy-seat Bristol FLF to East Bergholt outstation for peak-hour journeys to and from Colchester. For a few weeks this was FLF500 (MAH 500E), the only 1967-built FLF with a Gardner 6LX engine allocated to Ipswich. FLF500 was in Harwich Road, Mistley, in June 1970, working home to East Bergholt on the 17.15 221 service from Colchester.

The next departure on service 221 from Colchester was at 17.45 to East Bergholt, part of an East Bergholt outstation one-man duty. It was seen here in Harwich Road, Mistley, in June 1970, worked by LE995 (URB 559), a Bristol LS6G that was acquired from Midland General in 1968. She had retained thirty-nine coach seats in her Eastern Coach Works body.

Evening sunshine reflects off LFS93 (CVF 293B), a 1964-built Bristol FS5G, in Harwich Road, Mistley, in August 1970. LFS93 had worked the 17.45 Ipswich–Mistley 221 service, and was returning to Ipswich on the 18.45 departure from Mistley, which was part of an Ipswich instation crew duty.

Eastern Counties' first Bristol FLF6G arrived in 1966, and they all had Eastern Coach Works seventy-seat bodies. Numerically the first was FLF440 (GPW 440D). In June 1971 she was at East End Corner, Brantham, working from East Bergholt outstation on the 08.45 Colchester–Ipswich 221 service.

LS795 (4821 VF), a Bristol MW5G with an Eastern Coach Works thirty-nine seat coach body, was new in 1961. In June 1970, LS795 had just turned round at Rigby Avenue, Mistley, while working the 16.05 Colchester–Ipswich 221 service, which was part of the late crew duty at East Bergholt outstation.

Eastern Counties LM944 (3006 AH), a Bristol MW5G with an Eastern Coach Works forty-five-seat body, was new in 1959. In August 1970, LM944 was departing from Ipswich Old Cattle Market bus station on the 10.55 209 service to East Bergholt, which was part of an East Bergholt outstation one-man operated duty.

From the same batch as LS795, illustrated earlier, LS800 (4826VF) is seen at Ipswich Old Cattle Market bus station in July 1971 after conversion to one-man operation by Eastern Coach Works, but still retaining coach seats and coach livery. Next to LS800 is RLE869 (WPW 869H), a Bristol RELL6G with an Eastern Coach Works body with fifty semi-coach seats that was new in 1970 in coach livery.

LS805 (3805 PW) was new to Eastern Counties in 1962, a Bristol MW6G with thirty-two reclining coach seats in her Eastern Coach Works body for tour work. On a Saturday morning in July 1971, LS805 was at Ipswich Old Cattle Market bus station waiting to work an excursion to Norwich.

In 1967 Eastern Counties received fourteen Bristol RESL6Gs with five-speed manual gearboxes and Eastern Coach Works forty-six-seat bodies. RS655 (KVF 655E) is seen in Harwich Road, Mistley, in May 1970, working the 18.15 Ipswich–Clacton 123 service.

In 1968, the first Bristol RELL6Gs with Eastern Coach Works fifty-three-seat bodies arrived, starting the RL class. They had Gardner 6HLX engines and five-speed semi-automatic gearboxes. RL679 (RAH 679F) was working the 18.15 Ipswich–Clacton 123 service in Harwich Road, Mistley, in June 1971.

Eastern Counties RLC718 (WPW 718H) is seen in Castle Meadow, Norwich, in July 1971. She was a Bristol RELL6G with an Eastern Coach Works forty-eight-seat dual-door body, and was one of seven new in 1970 for Norwich city services. Revised Norwich city services were introduced with 5xx route numbers in 1971, and buses received new destination blinds with lower case lettering.

LH719 (NHU 100P) is seen at Surrey Street bus station, Norwich, in July 1971. LH719 was the prototype Bristol LH, chassis type LHX6P, which was new in 1968 with an Eastern Coach Works forty-five-seat body. It was acquired by Eastern Counties in 1970.

In 1971 a new numbering series started at RL501 for Bristol RELL6G buses with Eastern Coach Works bodies. RL507 (CNG 507K) is seen on layover at Ipswich Old Cattle Market bus station in October 1971 when she was only a few weeks old.

In 1970 Eastern Counties acquired five Bristol LHS6Ps with Eastern Coach Works thirty-seven-seat bodies from Luton Corporation, who had not operated them. In July 1975, LHS597 (WNG 103H), outstationed at East Bergholt, had worked the 17.45 Ipswich–Mistley 209 service, and was working home to East Bergholt on the 18.50 209 service from Mistley.

Eastern Counties LH534 (FNG 534K), a Bristol LH6P with an Eastern Coach Works forty-five-seat body, was new in 1972. In March 1976, LH534 was in Stutton, working service 221 from Ipswich to Mistley.

LM630 (FPW 630C), a Bristol MW5G with an Eastern Coach Works forty-five-seat body, was new in 1965. Allocated to Saxmundham depot, LM630 was at Ipswich Old Cattle Market bus station in April 1979, where it was about to move on to the departure stands to work the 16.35 264 service to Aldeburgh.

A friendly thumbs-up from the driver of LFS92 in Harwich Road, Mistley, in March 1978. LFS92 was working from East Bergholt outstation on the 16.35 209 Mistley–Ipswich service. LFS92 (CNG 292B) was a Bristol FS5G with an Eastern Coach Works sixty-seat body that was new to Eastern Counties in 1964.

RE881 (GNG 481C), a Bristol RELH6G with Eastern Coach Works forty-seven seat coach body, new in 1965. In May 1979, crew operated RE881 was at Colchester bus station, waiting to work the 15.30 Colchester–Ipswich 207 service instead of a Bristol Lodekka.

Eastern Counties RL680 (RAH 680F), a Bristol RELL6G with an Eastern Coach Works fifty-three-seat body, new in 1968, was regularly outstationed at Stradbroke. In June 1979, RL680 was on layover in Stradbroke after working the 10.35 Ipswich–Stradbroke 203 service.

Revised timetables and duties from 18 November 1979 saw the RL at Stradbroke outstation replaced by a VR. VR139 (SNG 439H), a Bristol VRT/SL2/6LX with an Eastern Coach Works seventy-four-seat body that was new in 1974, became the normal Stradbroke outstation bus. On 11 September 1981, VR139 had worked the 16.10 Ipswich–Stradbroke 273 service. The driver has opened the garage doors, and VR139 will be reversed into the garage for her overnight rest.

For many years rail passengers arriving at Cambridge railway station could complete their journey in to Cambridge on an Eastern Counties Bristol Lodekka. LFS54 (54 CPW), a Bristol FS5G that was new in 1963, was at Cambridge railway station on 8 April 1980, working city service 180 to Fen Estate via the city centre.

LFS109 (ENG 109C), a Bristol FS5G with an Eastern Coach Works sixty-seat body that was new in 1965, pulls out of Drummer Street bus station in Cambridge on 8 April 1980, working country service 103 to Pampisford.

In 1963 Eastern Counties received six Bristol FL6Bs with Eastern Coach Works seventy-seat bodies with open rear platforms. They spent most of their working lives on Norwich city services, but in April 1978 LFL58 (558 BNG) was working from Peterborough, and she was seen in the old bus station in Bishops Road, Peterborough. In 1972 LFL58 had received a Gardner 6LW engine, and platform doors had been fitted as well.

On 20 June 1980, FLF441 (GPW 441D) was on Market Hill in Woodbridge, working the 17.10 Ipswich–Aldeburgh 262 service. The FLF worked to Wickham Market and back. Saxmundham depot provided the connecting journeys to and from Aldeburgh. Crew operation at Ipswich depot finished on 3 January 1981 and the last two Bristol ECW Lodekkas at Ipswich, FLF440/441, were transferred to Norwich for further service.

In the National Bus Company/Scottish Bus Group Bristol FLF/VRT exchanges in 1973, Eastern Counties sent forty-six Bristol FLF6Gs, new in 1967/68, to Scotland, receiving thirty Bristol VRTs from Scotland and sixteen Bristol FLF6Gs from other National Bus Company subsidiaries. FLF423 (MVX 883C) was new to Eastern National in 1965 with fleet number 2846, and was one of six received from Eastern National. FLF423 was seen on 21 July 1981 at the combined bus station and depot at Great Yarmouth.

The other ten Bristol FLF6Gs came from Lincolnshire Road Car. One of these was 2716 (DFE 171D), which was new in 1966 and which became Eastern Counties FLF438. In April 1978 she was working a city service past the old bus station in Peterborough.

Eastern Counties FLF463 (KAH 463D) turns in to the new Queensgate bus station in Peterborough on 13 April 1982, working city service 384, Bretton–Westwood. On 31 December 1982, Bristol FLF and crew operation from Peterborough depot virtually finished, and from the next day Peterborough city services were revised and renumbered.

FLF475 (KPW 475D) is seen in Castle Meadow, Norwich, on 10 July 1982. In the background are two more Bristol/Eastern Coach Works Lodekkas working on city services. Crew operation and Bristol FLF operation came to an end in Norwich on 31 December 1983.

The first Bristol VRTs with a transverse rear engine to be built late in 1968 were twenty-five 33-foot-long Bristol VRT/LL6Gs with Eastern Coach Works eighty-three-seat bodies for Scottish Omnibuses (Eastern Scottish). Eastern Counties received twelve of these in 1973 as part of the National Bus Company/Scottish Bus Group Bristol FLF/VRT exchanges. VR310 (LFS 302F) was on Caister Road, Great Yarmouth, in August 1978.

VR383 (XVF 383J), a Bristol VRT/SL2/6LX with an Eastern Coach Works seventy-seat body, new in 1970. On 8 April 1980, VR383 was in Drummer Street bus station, Cambridge, looking very smart after a recent repaint.

From 1976 to 1981 the standard Eastern Counties double-decker was the Bristol VRT series, three of which had Eastern Coach Works seventy-four-seat bodies. Most had Gardner 6LXB engines and five-speed semi-automatic gearboxes. In August 1978, VR214 (BCL 214T) was nearing completion at the Eastern Coach Works factory in Lowestoft.

VR294 (VEX 294X) was the last Bristol VRT delivered to a National Bus Company subsidiary, in 1981. Bodied by Eastern Coach Works, Eastern Counties thoughtfully allocated VR294 to Lowestoft depot, where she was photographed on 22 June 1984. After withdrawal, VR294 was saved for preservation.

Eastern Counties received its first Leyland National integral single-deckers in 1972. LN587 (WAH 587S) was a type 11351A/1R with fifty-two seats and was new in 1977. In October 1977, LN587 had just passed her home depot of Felixstowe while working service 252, Ipswich–Felixstowe Dock.

Eastern Counties and London Country (Green Line) developed new limited-stop services – 797, 798 and 799 – between Cambridge and London Victoria. LL757 (SPW 103R), a Leyland Leopard PSU3E/4R with a Duple Dominant I body that was new in 1977, was working service 798 through Hoddesdon on 26 April 1981.

Eastern Counties RL709 (TPW 709G) was a Bristol RELL6G that was new in 1969, with the tall, flat windscreen on her Eastern Coach Works body. On 17 July 1981, RL709 was in St Andrews Street North in Bury St Edmunds, working a Bury St Edmunds town service.

RL739 (AAH 739J) was a Bristol RELL6G that was new in 1970. In May 1977, RL739 was working from Diss outstation, and is seen here at Ipswich Old Cattle Market bus station, loading up for her last journey of the day – the 18.05 851 service to Diss.

RE851 (SAH 851M) was a Bristol RELH6G with Plaxton Panorama Elite coachwork, which was new in 1974. When allocated to Ipswich, RE851 often worked on Eastline service 792, Ipswich–Peterborough. However, on 18 March 1983, RE851 had a break from Eastline 792, and is seen leaving Ipswich Old Cattle Market bus station on the 14.40 205 service to Sudbury.

Eastern Counties LH918 (TCL 138R), a Bristol LH6L with an Eastern Coach Works forty-three-seat body, was new in 1977. On 9 April 1980, LH918 was allocated to Saxmundham. She had just arrived at the combined bus station/depot there on service 269, which operated as a circular to and from Saxmundham via Rendham, Swefling and Bruisyard on Wednesdays, which was Saxmundham's market day.

The East Bergholt outstation of Eastern Counties closed on 3 January 1981, being replaced by a new location at Cattawade. There, on Sunday 11 January 1981, Bristol RELL6G RL728 (YPW 728J), which was new in 1970, and Bristol VRT/SL2/6LX VR138 (SNG438M), which was new in 1974, enjoyed a day of rest.

Service 123, Ipswich–Clacton, which was jointly operated by Eastern Counties and Eastern National, and was reinstated on 15 June 1981. On 28 November 1981, VR204 (XNG 204S), which was new in 1978 and was outstationed at Cattawade, worked the 12.35 Ipswich–Clacton 123 service. She was seen at the junction of Straight Road and Steam Mill Road in Bradfield. The square emblem to the left of the fleet name commemorated fifty years of Eastern Counties, 1931 to 1981.

Cattawade outstation closed on 11 June 1983, with the buses moving back to East Bergholt. The garage had been sold, so the buses parked on the forecourt, which is where, on 20 April 1984, RL507 (CNG 507K) and RLE869 (WPW 869H) are both seen. Both buses appear earlier in this book in Tilling liveries; here, they are in National Bus Company liveries.

RL687 (DRX 631K), a Bristol RELL6G with an Eastern Coach Works forty-nine-seat body, was new in 1972 and was acquired by Eastern Counties from Alder Valley in 1981. On 14 September 1985, RL687 was waiting for a driver change at Saxmundham bus station/depot while working service 80, Aldeburgh–Ipswich.

Winter sunshine catches the overall advert on VR256 (PCL 256W) on 28 December 1984. VR256 had worked the 08.40 Ipswich–Clacton 123 service as far as Mistley. By this time Eastern Counties worked Ipswich–Mistley and Eastern National worked Clacton–Mistley, and through passengers changed buses at Mistley (Rigby Avenue).

VR198 (TEX 408R) became the regular Sudbury outstation bus. VR198 was named *Thomas Gainsborough* after the artist (1727–1788), who was born in Sudbury. On 28 November 1987, VR198 passed through Stratford St Mary on service 92, Ipswich–Colchester. National Bus Company symbols had been removed, because Eastern Counties was privatised by a management buyout in February 1987.

Eastern Counties RLE871 (XAH 871H), a Bristol RELL6G with fifty semi-coach seats in her Eastern Coach Works body, is seen at Kettering bus station on 18 August 1982. Service 265, Peterborough–Kettering, was jointly operated by Eastern Counties and United Counties.

RL864 (WNG 864H) in Peterborough Queeensgate bus station on 21 April 1984, working from Kings Cliffe outstation. New as RLE864 in March 1970, she had been repainted into bus livery and was reclassified RL864, but the fifty comfortable semi-coach seats were retained.

Eastern Counties RLE873 (XAH 873H), new in July 1970, had the later style curved windscreen on her Eastern Coach Works body. Repainted into bus livery and reclassified RL873, the fifty semi-coach seats were retained. On 27 February 1982 RL873 was in St Stephens Street, Norwich, bound for Wymondham on service 813.

Eastline limited-stop service 790, Cambridge–Norwich–Great Yarmouth, commenced in 1982 using Leyland National 2 saloons, some of which gained this white and poppy red livery, but they retained bus seats. LN625 (UVF 625X) was on layover at Great Yarmouth depot on 25 August 1983.

The last Bristol REs delivered to Eastern Counties were eight RELH6Ls that were new in 1974 with Eastern Coach Works bus shell bodies fitted with forty-nine semi-coach seats. On 23 June 1983, RLE742 (GCL 344N) was working an Eastline 790 journey, Great Yarmouth–Cambridge, through Surrey Street bus station in Norwich.

The date is 21 April 1984, the Saturday of the Easter weekend, and Eastline service 790 was very busy. VR285 (VEX 285X), reseated from seventy-four bus seats to sixty-six semi-coach seats by Eastern Coach Works, was leaving Surrey Street bus station in Norwich with a good load of passengers for Great Yarmouth.

Eastern Counties RL744 (GCL 346N) turns into Queensgate bus station in Peterborough on 21 June 1984. New as RLE744 in 1974, she had been repainted into bus livery, but retained the forty-nine semi-coach seats. These eight Bristol RELH6Ls, numbered RLE740–747, had their Leyland engines replaced by Gardner 6HLX engines in 1980/81.

Two Bristol VRT/SL2/6LXs new to Ribble in 1972, and acquired by Eastern Counties in 1985, cross at Stowmarket market place on 11 August 1988. VR402 (OCK 990K) was departing for Ipswich, and VR382 (OCK 992K) was working service 88, Ipswich–Stowmarket–Harleston.

Eastern Counties LN599 (WVF 599S) was a standard 11.3-metre-long Leyland National 11351A/1R that was new in 1978. On 6 July 1987, LN599 was working from Saxmundham outstation, departing from Wickham Market on service 80, Ipswich–Aldeburgh.

Eastern Counties VR405 (KPW 405L) was a Bristol VRT/SL2/6LX that was new in 1973. On 18 April 1987, VR405 was working a Saturday duty from Framlingham outstation. VR405 had started her day's work on the 08.10 82 Framlingham–Ipswich service. In this photograph she was in Dogs Head Street, Ipswich, working her next journey, the 09.40 Ipswich–Aldeburgh 80 service.

CB813 (RCH 501R), a Bedford YRT with a Plaxton Supreme body, is seen at Diss bus park on 12 August 1988, working from Framlingham outstation on service 120, which operated on Fridays only – the Diss market day. RCH 501R was new to Barton Transport and was acquired by Eastern Counties with part of the Bickers of Coddenham business on 1 May 1988.

The Bristol VRT/SL3/6LXBs fitted with semi-coach seats in their Eastern Coach Works bodies received various liveries during their service with Eastern Counties. VR287 (VEX 287X) was parked at Framlingham outstation on 5 May 1991. The outstation building behind VR287 was occupied by two Leyland Nationals.

Second-hand series three Bristol VRTs acquired by Eastern Counties took fleet numbers left vacant by Bristol VRTs transferred to Cambus in 1984. The original VR186 (PEX 386R) became Cambus 712. The new VR186 was ODL 659R, which was acquired from Southern Vectis. She was seen here departing Ipswich Old Cattle Market bus station on 13 September 1991, working the 16.30 86 service to Stowupland.

The original VR250 (KVF 250V) became Cambus 737. The new VR250 was GRA 846V acquired from Trent, seen in Dogs Head Street, Ipswich, departing on the 17.05 81 service to Aldeburgh on Saturday 18 April 1992. At this time VR250 was outstationed at Bawdsey, where the driver worked a Monday to Friday duty, but on this Saturday he was helping out at Saxmundham outstation.

A number of Leyland National 1 saloons were converted to National Greenways. LN568 (PVF 368R) was at Wooodbridge (Turban Centre) on 16 July 1994, working the 14.40 Ipswich–Dennington 82 service. LN568 was later reclasssified LG568 because the National Greenway conversions received Gardner 6HLXB engines.

Eastern Counties did not receive their first Leyland Olympians until 1989, when five arrived with Gardner 6LXB engines and low-height Northern Counties bodies. On 27 May 1989, DD3 (F103 AVG) had paused opposite Felixstowe bus station while operating service 75, Ipswich–Felixstowe Dock.

Eastern Counties had two batches of new Dennis Javelins. S10 (G710 JAH) had Duple 300 bodywork. Allocated to Norwich when new, S10 was working service 25, Norwich–Bowthorpe, in West Earlham on 3 January 1990.

The second batch of Dennis Javelins had Plaxton Derwent bodies. S14 (H614 RAH) was operating from Saxmundham outstation on 26 May 1991, arriving in Framlingham on service 654 from Sizewell Nuclear Power Station Visitor Centre. This was one of a number of summer Sunday services sponsored by Suffolk County Council.

1993 brought a batch of five Dennis Lances with Cummins rear engines and Northern Counties Paladin bodies. Ipswich-allocated S36 (K736 JAH) was at Wickham Market on Sunday 10 April 1993, working service 80, Aldeburgh–Ipswich. This Sunday service was sponsored by Suffolk County Council, hence the 'County Connections' notice in the windscreen.

One of the first Bristol VRT/SL3/6LXBs at Ipswich depot to gain the Grampian Regional Transport cream-based livery was VR189 (RPW 189R). On 12 July 1995, VR189 was in Aldeburgh High Street, working from Saxmundham outstation on service 80, Ipswich–Aldeburgh.

A National Greenway conversion was LG588 (WAH 588S), originally Leyland National LN588, which was new in 1977. LG588 was at Thetford bus station on 7 October 1995, waiting to work back to Bury St Edmunds on service 131.

Two of the five Leyland Olympian/Northern Counties vehicles delivered in 1989 had coach seats for Eastline service 794, Peterborough–Kings Lynn–Norwich, and they were allocated to Kings Lynn. On 28 December 1994, OC4 (F104 AVG), reclassified from DD4, stood outside Kings Lynn depot.

Eastern National 1310 (215 MHK), a Bristol MW5G with an Eastern Coach Works body, was new in 1958. Allocated to Harwich, she was working the 17.50 Harwich–Manningtree 212 service in Harwich Road, Mistley, in May 1970. Through journeys from Harwich to Ipswich on service 212 were jointly operated by Eastern National and Eastern Counties.

Eastern National 1317 (212 MHK), a Bristol MW5G with an Eastern Coach Works forty-five-seat body, was new in 1959. Allocated to Clacton, 1317 picked up passengers at Stutton (Kings Head) in June 1970, working the 10.00 Clacton–Ipswich 123 service.

Eastern National 1423 (202 YVX), a Bristol MW5G with Eastern Coach Works body fitted with forty-one semi-coach seats, was new in 1962. In October 1970, 1423 was on loan from Colchester to Clacton, and was loading up at Ipswich Old Cattle Market bus station to work the 12.45 123 service to Clacton.

Eastern National 1505 (EPU 186G), a Bristol RELL6G with an Eastern Coach Works fifty-three-seat body, was new in 1969. Allocated to Clacton, 1505 was seen in Brantham working the 08.45 Clacton–Ipswich 123 service in June 1970.

Service 123 was revised to operate from Clacton to Manningtree from 30 April 1972, no longer being jointly operated with Eastern Counties. In August 1972, Eastern National 1246 (1861 F), a Bristol LS5G with an Eastern Coach Works forty-five-seat body that was new in 1957, had turned in to Heath Road, Mistley, working a Manningtree to Clacton service 123 journey.

2846 (MVX 883C) was a 1965-built Bristol FLF6G with an Eastern Coach Works seventy-seat body. Allocated to Harwich, she was working service 70, a Harwich–Colchester journey, in Harwich Road, Mistley, in February 1971. In 1973, 2846 was transferred to Eastern Counties, becoming FLF423. There is a photograph of FLF423 earlier in this book.

Eastern National 1434 (JHK 458C), a Bristol MW5G with an Eastern Coach Works body fitted with forty-three semi-coach seats, was new in 1965. In August 1971, 1423 had arrived at Harwich bus station on service 80 from Colchester. At this time service 80 connected at Colchester with Essex Coast Express coach services from London.

New to Tillings Transport in 1961, 1 BXB was a Bristol MW6G with an Eastern Coach Works coach body. Transferred to Eastern National in 1965, she was modified for bus work, fitted with forty-one bus seats, and converted to one-man operation in 1975. In this form, 1440 (1 BXB) was on loan from Clacton to Harwich in October 1977, and is seen parked outside Harwich depot.

Eastern National 2728 (175 XNO), a Bristol FLF6G with an Eastern Coach Works seventy-seat body, was new in 1961. In May 1977, 2728 was allocated to Harwich, and is pictured powering through Mistley on a Colchester to Harwich journey. Service 70, Colchester–Harwich, had been renumbered 103 as part of service revisions from 30 April 1972.

The spread of one-man operation gradually reduced the Bristol FLF Lodekkas at Harwich depot. 2842 (MVX 879C) was fresh from overhaul and repainting in April 1979. At that time she was the only Bristol FLF6G allocated to Harwich, working peak-hour journeys on Mondays to Fridays to and from Colchester on service 103.

Eastern National WNO 480 was a Bristol KSW5G with an Eastern Coach Works lowbridge body that was new in 1953. She was converted to highbridge open-top format and renumbered in 1965. In this form 2384 (WNO 480) was on layover in Clacton bus station on 24 August 1980.

Eastern National RHK 348D was new in 1966 as a standard Bristol/Eastern Coach Works FLF6B Lodekka. Her Bristol BVW engine was replaced by a Gardner 6LW in 1978. She was then converted to open top and was renumbered in 1979. In this form 2301 (RHK 348D) was about to depart from Clacton bus station on 30 August 1981.

3027 (NPU 974M) was a Bristol VRT/SL2/6LX that was new in 1973. Allocated to Harwich, she was seen working the 09.05 Colchester–Harwich 103 service in Harwich Road, Mistley, on 13 March 1982. In 1986, 3027 was converted to open top, and was renumbered 3501 for use on the Clacton open-top services.

3061 (LJN 656P) was a Bristol VRT/SL3 with a Leyland 501 engine and was new in 1975. On 27 March 1982, 3061 was leaving Colchester bus station on the 14.05 103 service to Harwich. Thus, for a period in 1981/82, Eastern National's Harwich depot had three different types of Bristol VRT: series one 3000, shown on the front cover of this book, series two 3027 and series three 3061.

3019 (SMS 45H) was a Bristol VRT/SL6G with an Eastern Coach Works body, and was one of fifteen new to W. Alexander & Sons (Midland) Ltd in 1970. In 1971 all fifteen came to Eastern National in exchange for Bristol FLF Lodekkas. On 27 March 1982, 3019 was allocated to Braintree, leaving Colchester bus station on the 15.05 70 service to Bishops Stortford.

3128 (XHK 233X) was a Bristol VRT/SL3/6LXB that was new in 1981, and was one of six diverted from Alder Valley to Eastern National. On 27 March 1982, Braintree-allocated 3128 swings off the stands in Colchester bus station, departing on service 70 to Bishops Stortford.

Following service 70 to its destination of Bishops Stortford, the Eastern National depot there was host to Chelmsford-allocated 1516 (FWC 439H) on 9 October 1981. 1516 was a Bristol RELL6G with an Eastern Coach Works fifty-three-seat body that was new in 1969. Today, 1516 is a very fine preserved bus, having been restored in original Tilling livery.

In 1977 Eastern National received four Bristol LH6Ls with Eastern Coach Works forty-three-seat bodies. They were allocated to Colchester for rural services. In March 1978, 1103 (UVX 7S) is seen about to move on to the departure stands at Colchester bus station in order to work service 75 to West Mersea on Mersea Island.

The Eastern Coach Works bus bodies on Bristol RE chassis changed during 1970, with the introduction of the curved windscreen design. Eastern National's first examples were Bristol RELL6Gs 1520 and 1521 (HTW 178/179H). In October 1977, 1520 was on loan from Clacton to Harwich, and is seen in Harwich Road, Mistley, working service 103, Harwich–Colchester.

From 1973 to 1980 Eastern National built up a large fleet of 11.3-metre-long Leyland Nationals. 1901 (DAR 123T) was only a few weeks old in April 1979 when she arrived at Harwich bus station on service 104 from Colchester.

1528 (LVX 116J) was a Bristol RELL6G with an Eastern Coach Works body and was new in 1970. On 1 July 1979, 1528 was allocated to Colchester. She was seen having just passed under Manningtree railway bridge, working summer Sunday service 87, Colchester–Dedham–East Bergholt–Flatford–Cattawade–Manningtree.

Two years later, on 12 July 1981, summer Sunday service 87 was worked by Colchester-allocated 1053 (TJN 976W), a Bedford YMQS with a Wadham Stringer body fitted with thirty-three coach-type seats. 1053 was only a few weeks old at the time of this photograph. 1053 was using the level crossing for vehicles over 10 feet high, which was adjacent to Manningtree railway bridge.

On 15 June 1981, service 123, Clacton–Ipswich, was reinstated, once again being jointly operated by Eastern National and Eastern Counties. On 25 June 1982, Clacton-allocated Leyland National 1825 (VAR 902S) had arrived at Dogs Head Street in Ipswich, working the 08.40 Clacton–Ipswich 123 service.

Bristol RELL6G 1523 (KHK 415J) was new in 1970. On 19 June 1982, 1523 was waiting in the Old Cattle Market bus station in Ipswich before departing for home on the 16.35 123 service to Clacton. 1523 was in overall leaf green livery following the National Bus Company's decision to eliminate the white band on single-deck buses.

Eastern National 1205 (BNO 691T) was a Bedford YMT with Duple Dominant II coachwork that was new in 1978. Allocated to Braintree, 1205 is seen leaving Ipswich Old Cattle Market bus station on 19 June 1982, working National Express service 133 from Great Yarmouth to Southend.

1419 (GJD 195N) was a Bristol RELH6L with Plaxton Supreme coachwork, and was new to National Travel South East in 1975. Transferred to Eastern National in 1979, 1419 was refurbished and later fitted with a Gardner 6HLX engine. On 28 May 1983, Harwich-allocated 1419 was in Dogs Head Street, Ipswich, working Highwayman service 814 from Harwich and Clacton to Cromer and Sheringham.

Eastern National 1131 (C131 HJN), a Leyland Tiger TRCTL11/3RH with Plaxton Paramount coachwork, was only a few weeks old on 29 March 1986, when she was photographed at Drummer Street bus station in Cambridge. She was working Highwayman service 801, Chelmsford–Kings Lynn.

1123 (A692 OHJ), a Leyland Tiger TRCTL11/2R with an Alexander TE dual-purpose body, was new in 1983. On 28 May 1989, 1123 was working from Harwich depot on summer Sunday service 687, Colchester–Manningtree. 1123 is pictured near East Bergholt church, having just negotiated the narrow road to serve Flatford in the heart of Constable country, made famous by the paintings of John Constable (1776–1837).

4006 (C712 HEV) was a Leyland Olympian ONLXB/1R with an Eastern Coach Works body, and was new in 1985. On 9 March 1991, 4006 was working from Harwich depot. She is pictured arriving at Harwich bus station, with the destination display already set for the next journey to Colchester on service 104.

There were fifteen Leyland Olympian ONLXB/1Rs delivered in 1986 with Eastern Coach Works bodies fitted with seventy-two semi-coach seats instead of seventy-seven bus seats. Therefore, they received the dual-purpose version of the new livery. On 8 March 1986, 4007 (C407 HJN) was only a few weeks old, and is seen leaving Colchester bus station on service 103, working back to her home depot of Harwich.

Eastern National 3030 (NPU 977M), a Bristol VRT/SL2/6LX with an Eastern Coach Works seventy-seat body, was new in 1973. On 2 April 1988 she was parked in Walton-on-the-Naze garage, which was an outstation of Clacton depot.

Eastern National became part of the Badgerline Group in 1990. 3219 (VTH 941T) was a Bristol VRT/SL3 with a Leyland 501 engine and was acquired from South Wales Transport, another member of the Badgerline Group. On 9 March 1991, 3219 was parked outside Harwich depot. By this time fleet number plates had been replaced by black transfers, but depot allocation plates were still carried.

Eastern National standard 11.3-metre-long Leyland National 1885 (BNO 675T) was new in 1978. On 29 September 1990, she was leaving Harwich bus station, working local service 120 to Parkeston Quay. By this time, new destination blinds showing via points had been fitted.

1927 (MHJ 723V) was a Leyland National 2 NL116L11/1R (11.6 metres long) and was new in 1980. Allocated to Colchester, 1927 was in Colchester High Street, near the end of her journey from Chelmsford on service 53, on 5 April 1994.

In 1988 Eastern National received thirty Leyland Lynx integral single-deckers with forty-nine seats. On 30 September 1988, 1416 (F416 MWC) was waiting for departure time in Colchester bus station in order to return to her home depot of Maldon.

Badgerline ownership brought a new yellow and green livery, complete with a smiling badger emblem. The Dennis Dart with Plaxton Pointer body was a standard Badgerline bus. Colchester-allocated 819 (L819 OPU) was on layover outside Harwich depot on 15 July 1994. At this time Colchester had one vehicle duty on services 103/104, Harwich–Colchester. All other duties were worked by Harwich depot.

Eastern National 3223 (MFA 721V) was a Bristol VRT/SL3 with a Leyland 501 engine and was acquired in 1994 from Potteries Motor Traction, another member of the Badgerline Group. Her Eastern Coach Works body had sixty-seven semi-coach seats. Allocated to Colchester, 3223 was leaving Colchester bus station on service 78 for Brightlingsea on 13 July 1995.

Harwich-allocated 1125 (A694 OHJ) was a Leyland Tiger with an Alexander TE dual-purpose body that was new in 1983. She is pictured in Harwich Road, Mistley, on 16 July 1995. Service 102 was the Sunday variation of service 104, Colchester–Harwich, which also served Dedham and Parkeston.

United Counties 662 (ABD 662B), a Bristol FS6B with an Eastern Coach Works body, was new in 1964. She was resting at Cambridge railway station on 28 June 1980 having worked to Cambridge on the long 128 service from Northampton. The blue fleet number plate denoted her allocation to the Bedford depot.

281 (TBD 281G), a Bristol RELH6G new in 1969, had an Eastern Coach Works bus bodyshell fitted with forty-nine semi-coach seats. On 4 July 1981, 281 was on layover in the old Peterborough bus station having worked service 230, Huntingdon–Warboys–Ramsey–Peterborough, which was jointly operated with Eastern Counties.

United Counties 225 (MRP 225P) was a Leyland Leopard PSU3C/4R with an Alexander body and was new in 1976. On 27 October 1984, 225 was in Lowestoft bus station prior to working National Express service 747 to Northampton.

A typical scene in St Andrews Street, Cambridge, with cyclists and pedestrians mixing with buses on 8 October 1986. United Counties 762 (VNV 762H), a Bristol VRT/SL2/6LX with an Eastern Coach Works body, was new in 1970, and was on hire to Cambus at that time.

In 1980 the inter-urban services of Lincolnshire Road Car were revised and branded Fenlander. The long-standing service 65, Spalding–Kings Lynn, was renumbered 505. On 8 January 1983, 1914 (NVL 992K), a Bristol VRT/SL2/6LX with an Eastern Coach Works body that was new in 1972, was loading up in Kings Lynn bus station for a return journey to Spalding.

On 31 July 1982 Lincolnshire Road Car 1920 (MVL 130P), a Bristol VRT/SL3/6LX with Eastern Coach Works body that was new in 1976, was on layover in Kings Lynn bus station. Service 505, Spalding–Kings Lynn, was operated from a depot at Holbeach.

Another long Fenlander service was 507, Skegness–Boston–Spalding–Peterborough, with Eastern Counties drivers working between Spalding and Peterborough. On 28 September 1984, Lincolnshire Road Car 1963 (SVL 173W), a Bristol VRT/SL3/6LXB that was new in 1981, was on layover in Peterborough.

Great Yarmouth Corporation Transport bought Leyland Atlanteans before the Colchester or Ipswich municipal operations did. 5 (AEX 5B), with bodywork by C. H. Roe, was new in 1964. She was seen in Caister Road, Great Yarmouth, in August 1978.

Great Yarmouth Corporation Transport built up a fleet of AEC Swifts. 60 (LEX 860H), new in 1970, had a Willowbrook dual-door body with forty-three seats, and is seen leaving the Caister Road depot in August 1978.

Later AEC Swifts had Eastern Coach Works dual-door bodywork with forty-three seats. 89 (WEX 689M) was new in 1973. She was photographed at South Denes, Great Yarmouth, in August 1978.

Waveney (Lowestoft) Borough Transport ceased operations in 1977. Lowestoft had also bought AEC Swifts with Eastern Coach Works dual-door bodies, but with flat windscreens. Great Yarmouth bought the newest two from Waveney. One of these, 92 (NRT 565L), was at North Denes, Great Yarmouth, in August 1978.

Later double-deckers in the Great Yarmouth fleet were Bristol VRT/SL3/6LXBs with Eastern Coach Works bodies. New in 1981, 26 (PVG 26W) was at Wellington Pier, Great Yarmouth, on 19 August 1982.

Colchester Borough Transport 43 (OVX 143D), a Leyland Titan PD2A/30 with a Massey body, is seen in Colchester bus station, March 1978. When new in 1966, 43 had an open platform, but was later fitted with platform doors.

56 (JHK 496N), a Leyland Atlantean AN68/1R with an Eastern Coach Works body, was new in 1975. She was seen in Colchester bus station on 5 September 1981. This style of bodywork was also built on Daimler Fleetline chassis supplied to South Yorkshire PTE.

Colchester Borough Transport 84 (MEV 84V), a Leyland Atlantean AN68A/1R that was new in 1979, had the more common style of Eastern Coach Works body with the curved windscreen. On 30 May 1982, 84 was in Burrell Road, Ipswich, approaching Ipswich railway station on a rail replacement service from Colchester.

When Leyland Atlantean production ceased, Colchester Borough Transport bought the Leyland Olympian, also with Eastern Coach Works bodywork. 42 (C42 HHJ), new in 1985, had chassis type ONLXCT/1RH. She was seen leaving Thorpe-le-Soken railway station on a rail replacement service on 26 March 1989.

Colchester Borough Transport bought fifteen Bristol RELL6Ls with Eastern Coach Works bodies. 28 (SWC 28K), new in 1972, was awaiting a driver change in Osborne Street, Colchester, on 26 September 1981.

Later single-deckers were Leyland Lynxes. Numerically the first was 31 (D31 RWC), which was new in 1985 with a Leyland TL11 engine. On 1 May 1988, 31 had negotiated the narrow road through Wrabness village to serve Wrabness railway station while working a Harwich to Manningtree rail replacement service.

Ipswich Borough Transport 61 (SDX 61) was an AEC Regent V 2D2RA with an AEC Monocontrol semi-automatic transmission and an East Lancashire body. She was new in 1963 and is pictured at Tower Ramparts bus station in Ipswich on 19 June 1981. The Electric House destination, instead of Tower Ramparts, persisted for many years, maintaining a link to Ipswich Corporation's history of operating electric trams and trolleybuses.

Batches of new AEC Regent Vs replaced most of Ipswich's trolleybuses. Years later the AEC Regent Vs were replaced mainly by Leyland Atlanteans. 22 (SDX 22R) was a Leyland Atlantean AN68A/1R with a C. H. Roe body and was new in 1977. She was seen in Stoke Park, Ipswich, on 15 October 1983.

When Eastern Counties withdrew the Sunday service on route 202, Ipswich–Shotley, Ipswich Borough Transport took over. The Ipswich Borough concessionary fare for senior citizens was valid, so this Sunday service became very popular, needing double-deck capacity. 40 (RGV 40W), a Leyland Atlantean AN68C/1R with an East Lancashire body, was new in 1981. She had just crossed Bourne Bridge, leaving Ipswich for Shotley on 25 July 1982.

78 (JRT 78K), an AEC Swift with a Willowbrook dual-door forty-seat body that was new in 1971, was seen at Ellenbrook Green in Ipswich on 30 April 1983. Ipswich Borough Transport needed single-deckers for services 12/13 to the Chantry Estate, which passed under the low railway bridge in Ancaster Road.

The next batch of AEC Swifts for Ipswich Borough Transport had East Lancashire dual-door forty-seat bodywork. 93 (DDX 93L) was new in 1973. She was seen at Tower Ramparts bus station on 9 March 1985.

Later, Ipswich Borough Transport bought batches of Dennis Falcons, which had Gardner 6HLXB rear engines. 101 (YDX 101Y), with an East Lancashire forty-four-seat dual-door body and new in 1983, is seen in Cambridge Drive on the Chantry Estate on 2 April 1983.

In 1980 Ipswich Borough Transport bought five Bristol RELL6Ls from Leicester City Transport. They were new in 1969 and had Eastern Coach Works dual-door forty-seven-seat bodywork. The Ipswich livery suited them very well. 119 (TRY 119H) was crossing Stoke Bridge in Ipswich on 19 June 1982.

The Leyland B21 was an export model, but Ipswich Borough Transport acquired four in 1985 after an export order was cancelled. They were bodied by Alexander (Belfast). 147 (B117 LDX) was leaving East Bergholt High School on a school contract on 3 July 1992. Note the Bristol nameplate and 'Bristolian' name, because the Leyland B21 was built at the Bristol Commercial Vehicle factory in Brislington, Bristol.

The buses of Bickers of Coddenham became a more common sight in Ipswich in 1974, when Bickers took over services from Ipswich to Debenham and Otley that were withdrawn by Eastern Counties. Bickers BDV 244C was a Bristol SUL4A with an Eastern Coach Works thirty-six-seat body and was new to Western National in 1965. She was seen on layover at Ipswich Old Cattle Market on 11 October 1980, having worked in on service 8 from Otley.

Bickers NPT 992M, an AEC Reliance with a Plaxton Derwent body, was new to Gillet Brothers of Quarrington Hill in 1973. On 22 August 1980, NPT 992M was waiting to depart from the Blue Coat Boy at Ipswich Old Cattle Market on service 9 to Debenham.

Bickers RBD 105M was a Bedford YRT with a Willowbrook body and was new to United Counties in 1974. On 28 December 1984, she was in Debenham, working service 9 to Ipswich.

Bickers UFT 928T, a Bedford YMT with Plaxton Supreme IV coachwork, was new in 1979 to Rochester and Marshall. On 30 April 1988, she was in Bawdsey, working service 16 from Ipswich. This was the last day of Bickers operating local bus services, which were taken over by Eastern Counties and Ipswich Buses. The Ipswich–Bawdsey service had moved from Eastern Counties to Bickers on 7 June 1982, but with the Bickers takeover it returned to Eastern Counties from 3 May 1988.

Norfolk's of Nayland operated into Ipswich on Fridays and Saturdays, and for many years their terminus was Neale Street, to the north of Tower Ramparts bus station. On 19 April 1980, the Stoke-by-Nayland to Ipswich service was worked by YCE 675L, an AEC Reliance 6U3ZR with a Plaxton Panorama Elite body, which had been new to Burwell & District in 1973, and was acquired by Norfolk's in 1979.

On layover in Colchester bus station on 23 June 1984, Norfolk's of Nayland NWU 324M was a Bristol RELL6G with an Eastern Coach Works body. She was new to West Yorkshire Road Car Company in 1973, and was acquired by Norfolk's in 1983.

H. C. Chambers & Son of Bures operated a long stage carriage service from Colchester to Bury St Edmunds. On 7 October 1986, C688 WRT, a Bedford YMT with a Duple Dominant bus body, which was new in the same year, collected passengers at Sudbury bus station.

H. C. Chambers & Son G864 XDX was a Leyland Olympian ONCL10/1RZ with a Cummins L10 engine and an Alexander low-height body. She was new in 1989. On 21 July 1990, she was on layover in Colchester bus station after working in from Bury St Edmunds.

Hedingham & District L118 (KHK 414J) was a Bristol RELL6G with an Eastern Coach Works body, and was new to Eastern National in 1970 with fleet number 1522. On 2 April 1988, L118 was in Sudbury bus station, working the ex-Eastern National service 328 from Great Cornard to Sudbury.

Hedingham & District L150 (F150 LTW), a Leyland Lynx with a Cummins L10 engine, was new in 1988. On 1 October 1988, L150 was leaving Colchester bus station on service 88 to Halstead, a route shared with Eastern National.

Carters Coach Services started their first stage carriage service on 2 August 1985, a Fridays-only service 247 from East Bergholt (East End) to Colchester. On 13 September 1985, PPM 206G, a Bristol RESL6G with an Eastern Coach Works dual-door body, was new in 1968 to Brighton, Hove & District. She was seen collecting passengers in Colchester bus station.

Service 247 developed in to a Monday to Saturday operation, with Saturday journeys serving Lawford. On 2 April 1988, Carters XAH 872H, a Bristol RELL6G with an Eastern Coach Works body, new in 1970 to Eastern Counties as RLE872, has just passed under the low railway bridge at Manningtree railway station.

Service 755, East Bergholt–Hadleigh–Colchester, was a Suffolk County Council tendered service. On 19 November 1994, Carters SVW 274K, a Bristol RELL6G with an Eastern Coach Works body, which was new to Eastern National in 1972 with fleet number 1546, picked up passengers in Polstead, Suffolk. SVW 274K is now a preserved bus, having been restored in National Bus Company livery.

Carters NNO 61P, a Leyland Atlantean AN68A/1R with an Eastern Coach Works body, was new to Colchester Borough Transport in 1976. On 13 September 1991, NNO 61P was seen in Tattingstone, working the 17.40 Ipswich–Bentley 94 service – a Suffolk County Council tendered journey.

Visits to Peterborough were enhanced by seeing the immaculate fleet of Delaine Coaches of Bourne. In April 1978, 60 (DTL 489D), a Leyland Atlantean PDR1/2 with a Willowbrook body, which was bought new in 1966, was on layover in the old Bishop's Road bus station in Peterborough while working the Bourne–Peterborough service.

Delaine 102 (GDB 181N), a Leyland Atlantean AN68/1R with a Northern Counties body, was new in 1975 to Greater Manchester Transport, and was acquired by Delaine in 1987. On 21 September 1989, 102 was leaving Peterborough for Bourne.

Delaine 107 (YPD 107Y), a Leyland Tiger with a Duple Dominant IV body, was new to London Country in 1983 for Green Line services. She was acquired by Delaine in 1989. On 27 August 1994, 107 was collecting passengers in Queensgate bus station, Peterborough, working the Peterborough–Barnack–Stamford service that Delaine took over from Barton Transport in April 1988.

In February 1995 Delaine took delivery of two new long-wheelbase Volvo Olympians with East Lancashire bodies. On 11 July 1995, the second of the two, 117 (M2 OCT), was leaving Queensgate bus station in Peterborough on the service to Bourne.

Premier Travel GER 501E, an AEC Reliance 2U3RA with an Alexander Y-type body with forty-nine coach seats, was new in 1967. In August 1978, GER 501E was outside the Eastern National depot at Station Approach, Harwich. At this time express service 5, Birmingham–Clacton, was extended to Dovercourt and Harwich during the summer months.

Premier Travel CJE 452V, a Leyland Leopard PSU3F/4R with a Plaxton Supreme body, was new in 1980. On 25 August 1986, CJE 452V collected passengers at Stowmarket market place while working the 09.10 Ipswich–Peterborough Eastline limited-stop 792 service.

When Eastern Counties was split up on 9 September 1984, coaching work passed to Ambassador Travel. On 6 April 1985, Ambassador Travel ex-Eastern Counties LL805 (LCL 805V), a Leyland Leopard PSU3E/4R with a Duple Dominant II body, which was new in 1980, departed from Ipswich Old Cattle Market bus station working the 07.40 Peterborough–Felixstowe Eastline 792 service. At that time this service was jointly operated by Ambassador Travel and Premier Travel.

Ambassador Travel/ex-Eastern Counties LL880 (CAH 880Y), a Leyland Leopard PSU3G/4R with an Eastern Coach Works body, which was new in 1982, was at Ipswich Old Cattle Market bus station on 8 April 1985. The destination blind was set for National Express service 783, Cardiff–Ipswich.

Cambus took over the western area of Eastern Counties' operations on 8 September 1984. The first Bristol VRT to receive Cambus livery was ex-Eastern Counties VR209 (YNG 209S), which became Cambus 719. This Bristol VRT/SL3/6LXB was new in 1978, and was seen at Newmarket depot on 22 September 1984.

Another early repaint into Cambus livery was ex-Eastern Counties RL504 (BVF 667J), a Bristol RELL6G that was new in 1971. She was on layover in Peterborough on 28 September 1984. Later, she was renumbered 115 in the Cambus fleet.

Cambus 601 (FRB 213H) was seen in Drummer Street bus station in Cambridge on 5 June 1985. This Bristol VRT/SL2/6LX with an Eastern Coach Works body was new to Mansfield & District in 1970. She became VR382 in the Eastern Counties fleet in 1982.

Cambus inherited two Bristol LH6Ls with Eastern Coach Works bodies, which were new in 1977, from Eastern Counties. Cambus 81 (WEX 924S), ex-Eastern Counties LH924, was in St Andrews Street, Cambridge, on 30 August 1986.

Cambus 207 (GCL 341N) was seen in Emmanuel Street, Cambridge, on 5 June 1985, working cross-city service 190 from Bar Hill to Cherry Hinton. 207 was a standard 11.3-metre-long Leyland National 11351/1R, and was new in 1974 as Eastern Counties LN557.

The eight Bristol RELH6Ls (later RELH6G) with Eastern Coach Works bodies that were new to Eastern Counties in 1974 all passed to Cambus. RLE747 (GCL 349N) became Cambus 158, and was seen in St Andrews Street, Cambridge, on 30 August 1986. She is now preserved, having been restored as Eastern Counties RLE747 in National white livery.

Various second-hand Bristol VRTs entered the Cambus fleet over the years. Here is 629 (RKO 819M), which was seen in St Andrews Street, Cambridge, on 8 October 1986. She was a Bristol VRT/SL2/6LX that was new to Maidstone & District in 1974. She was transferred to Hastings & District in 1983, and was acquired by Cambus in 1984.

800 (OBN 511R) was a Leyland Fleetline FE30AGR with a Northern Counties body and was new to Lancashire United Transport in 1977, being one of a number of Fleetlines acquired by Cambus from Greater Manchester Buses in 1987. On 18 April 1987, 800 was in service at the Cowley Road, Cambridge, Park and Ride site.

On Sunday 24 July 1988, Cambus organised an event to celebrate the eighty-fifth anniversary of Peterborough Electric Traction Company – one of the constituents of Eastern Counties. This event included half-cab double-deckers working Peterborough city services. Cambus 50 (BNG 886B), a Bristol FS5G new to Eastern Counties in 1964 as LFS86, was at Orton Wistow on cross-city service 53 to Werrington.

Also in service in Peterborough on 24 July 1988 was Cambus 61 (JAH 553D), a Bristol FLF6G that was new to Eastern Counties in 1966 as FLF453. Repainted into Tilling red livery, 61 was at Yaxley on cross-city service 52 to Welland.

Cambus 403 (OEX 798W) was leaving Drummer Street bus station in Cambridge on 18 April 1987, working limited-stop service 797 to London Victoria, which was jointly operated with London Country (Green Line). 403 was a Leyland Leopard PSU3E/4R with a Willowbrook body, and was new to Eastern Counties as LL798 in 1980.

Cambus 415 (JVF 815V) has paused at Stevenage on 24 March 1988, also working on limited-stop service 797. 415 was a Leyland Leopard PSU3E/4R with Plaxton Supreme IV coachwork, and was new to Eastern Counties as LP815 in 1979.

Some Bristol RELL6Gs with Eastern Coach Works bodies lasted in the Cambus fleet long enough to receive the revised livery. Sixteen-year-old 120 (EPW 516K) was seen leaving Queensgate bus station in Peterborough on 5 January 1988. Now a preserved bus, she has been restored as Eastern Counties RL516 in National Bus Company livery.

Cambus 748 (STW 30W) was a Bristol VRT/SL3/6LXB that was new to Eastern National in 1981 with fleet number 3086. She served with Cambus from 1991 to 1996. On 14 April 1993, 748 was in St Andrews Street North, Bury St Edmunds, operating service 177 to Soham.

In 1988 and 1989, Cambus purchased twelve new Leyland Olympian ONLXB/1RZs with low-height Northern Counties bodies. On 28 June 1989, 516 (F516 NJE) had reversed off the stands in the rebuilt Drummer Street bus station in Cambridge, working service 111 to Newmarket.

In 1993 Cambus bought fourteen 8.5-metre-long Volvo B6s with Marshall thirty-two seat bodies. 164 (L664 MFL) was photographed in Arbury, Cambridge, on 25 October 1993.

Viscount B52 (VEX 299X) was a standard Bristol VRT/SL3/6LXB that was new in 1981 to Eastern Counties as VR299 – one of ten such diverted from United Counties. Later numbered 752 in the Cambus fleet, B52 was in Queensgate bus station, Peterborough, on 21 September 1989.

Viscount B60 (VAH 280X), an early repaint into Viscount livery, was seen in March town centre on 21 September 1989. She was new to Eastern Counties as VR280, and was later, when with Cambus, renumbered to 750. She was built in 1981 – the last year of VRT production by Bristol and Eastern Coach Works.

Another early repaint into the new Viscount livery was Leyland National 2 B20 (PEX 620W), which was seen standing at the entrance to Lincoln Road depot in Peterborough on 21 September 1989. She was new to Eastern Counties as LN620 in 1981, and was then renumbered 304 in the Cambus fleet in 1984.

Viscount B64 (YWY 830S) was seen in Queensgate bus station in Peterborough on 20 July 1990. She was a Bristol VRT/SL3/6LXB that was new in 1978 to West Yorkshire Road Car Co., who had adopted this Tilling Red livery upon privatisation. YWY 830S had transferred to York City & District when West Yorkshire Road Car Co. was split up in 1989. She was then acquired by Viscount in 1990.

In 1990 Viscount bought three new Leyland Olympians with Gardner engines and Leyland bodies to the Eastern Coach Works design. B3 (H473 CEG), named *Sir Henry Royce Bt*, was leaving Queensgate bus station in Peterborough on 23 November 1990. Henry Royce was born in Alwalton, near Peterborough, in 1863. In 1906 he founded Rolls-Royce Ltd with Charles Rolls.

Viscount T12 (E502 LFL) was a Leyland Olympian with a Gardner 6LXCT engine and Optare bodywork to the Eastern Coach Works design. She was new to Cambus as 502 in 1988. She was renumbered by Viscount in the T series for travel/coaches, because she had seventy coach seats. On 11 July 1995, T12 was passing the Rose and Crown in Oundle on the long X65 service from Peterborough to Northampton.

Bibliography

Carter, Paul, *Cambridge 2 1950–1986* (Venture Publications Ltd).

Cobb, Stephen, *Ipswich Buses – An Illustrated History* (Ipswich Buses Ltd).

Collins, R. N. and Mills, G. R., *From Trams to Arriva in Colchester Essex 1904–2004* (MW Transport Publications).

Delaine-Smith, A., *The Delaine History Part 2 1983–1990* (Delaine Coaches Ltd).

Palmer, Bob, *Eastern National Fleet Record Volume 1: 1964–1990* (Essex Bus Enthusiasts Group).

Eastern Counties Fleet History (PSV Circle, Omnibus Society and Eastern Counties Omnibus Society).

Fleet History of Ambassador Travel, Cambus and Viscount (PSV Circle).

Ipswich Transport Society Journals (Ipswich Transport Society).

PSV Circle News Sheets (PSV Circle).

Essex Bus News magazines (Essex Bus Enthusiasts Group).

Terminus magazines (Eastern Counties Omnibus Society, now Eastern Transport Collection Society).

http://bcv.robsly.com/ – Bristol Commercial Vehicles Enthusiasts by Rob Sly.